The Bird Hour

Also by Kim Antieau

The Bird Hour

Kim Antieau

Green Snake
PUBLISHING

The Bird Hour
by Kim Antieau

Copyright © 2024 by Kim Antieau

ISBN: 978-1-949644-85-2

Cover and interior illustrations created by Kim
Antieau from her photos.

Book design by Kim Antieau and Mario Milosevic

Thanks to Nancy Milosevic

Published by Green Snake Publishing
www.greensnakepublishing.com

Contents

On the Wing

Sometimes we need a little help from our friends—or we need help from our winged neighbors: birds. If you are seeking some relief from the chaos of the world, if you are searching for a method to help you focus and ease your anxiety, or if you want an excuse to be with Nature at least an hour a day, read on. The Bird Hour may be the answer.

The Bird Hour is one hour where you don't have to do anything ex-

Pileated Woodpecker

cept watch and listen for birds. It is one hour where you don't think about anything except birds. You don't need to know anything about birds. Or you can know a lot about birds. Anyone can participate in the Bird Hour. All you need for the Bird Hour is yourself, ready and willing to watch or listen to the wild.

Call of the Birds

I am so lucky. I can sit in my office and watch the birds just outside my window. An old palo verde and an old mesquite tree are wrapped around each other just feet from my window. They provide shade and food in a place that is often dangerously hot. I've put out benches and water, so the area is visited all day long and into the night by wildlife.

Birds evolved from theropod dinosaurs around 165–150 million years ago, during the Jurassic period. Humans evolved 6 to 2 million years ago. Wow! Compared with birds, we are babies on this planet.

The birds are mostly gone at night, but our trail camera has photographed a tiny Western Screech Owl at the watering stations several times—along with bobcats, coyotes,

badgers, javelinas, raccoons, and rabbits. Mostly in the day time, the place is busy with birds. Right now five Gambel's Quail are picking at the dirt or sharing water with a squirrel. A gorgeous black Phainopepla is perched in the palo verde tree, waiting for his chance at the water tray. A Green-tailed Towhee just drank from one of the water trays, and now one of the Gambel's Quail is kicking up dirt as she digs a cool place to rest.

Bald Eagle

I could watch all day long.

The window is a perfect blind; as long as I don't make too much of a shadow when I get close to the glass, the birds ignore me. If I feel like the world is going to hell in a handbasket, I can watch birds from my office, even if it's 110° outside. I prefer being out of doors, but I live in Arizona, and that's not always possible.

Recently, as the pandemic seemed to be shifting into COVID becoming endemic, I shifted into a major depression with high anxiety. I have chronic depression and anxiety, but the levels are usually something I can manage. The pandemic hit mere months after we moved from Washington state to Arizona, and I did not do very well. As everyone seemed to forget the pandemic and what happened during the worst of it, I felt more and more anxious.

That's when I decided to start the Bird Hour. I've never been able to do formal meditation for very long. Other stress-reduction exercises often don't work for me. Being mindful for me often means a thousand things are running around in my head, all of them yammering to be heard. That is not relaxing.

When I write—especially when I'm writing fiction—the anxiety usually fades away. My mind is able to focus on one thing. But I wasn't writing. My anxiety and depression were just too bad. I needed help.

Being in nature and looking and listening for birds often calmed me—until I started worrying about chores at home or the state of the world or my husband. I knew if I could just focus on one thing—like I did when writing—things would probably improve for me. But I needed to force myself to do one thing. Essentially I needed an excuse not to worry. I love Nature. What in Nature do I encounter every day? Birds!

Arizona has a lot of birds and lots of varieties of birds. So that was it. Perfect! I decided I would concentrate on birds for an hour, and I would think about only one thing during that time: birds. This would give my monkey mind something to do besides be anxious and depressed. When I told

Mario about the Bird Hour, he asked if he could join me, and I happily said yes.

First we figured out our rules for the Bird Hour. We would sit or walk and watch for birds, listen for birds, and look up information in our bird books (if we wanted). We couldn't talk about chores, politics, the state of the world, or anything besides birds. And if we had our phones, they had to be on airplane mode.

We had the first hour on the patio of the Ca-sita. The Casita has an at-

Red-naped Sapsucker

tached garage (to our house) that had been converted into a lovely studio apartment by the former owners. In the winter, we rented it out to travelers. The rest of the year, we used it as a writing or sleeping space. The birds loved the old mesquite at the center of the walled garden.

The Bird Hour was immediately healing for me. Having a break in the constant stream of anxiety began to calm my body. I did the Bird Hour every day for a while. I wasn't suddenly cured of all of what ailed me. But I was able to get through the summer and beyond. I actually learned a lot about birds during that first Bird Hour summer, but that was just a bonus. Mostly my nervous system calmed down a bit, and life felt more livable.

In the beginning, I wrote about many of our Bird Hours. After a while, I didn't feel the need to document it. I could just "be" in the hour. It had no purpose beyond me being with the birds. That was it. I didn't need to learn more about the birds—even though I did. I needed to have the experience of actually moving away from anxiety and into Nature in a more direct way. I was purposely shutting off my troubles and watching birds. I didn't think I would be able to do it at first—to not be anxious for an hour—but I did it. And I did it again and again.

Now Mario and I will say to each other, "Let's do Bird Hour" and it doesn't always mean we're watching for an hour, but it does mean nothing else goes on during that time except birds: we are listening, we are watching, and we are talking about birds.

Me and Birds

When I was a girl growing up in the country outside of a small town in southeast Michigan, birds were my constant companions, along with the oak trees I climbed and the woods I ran through. The yearly routines of birds were a part of my yearly routines. In the fall thousands of them gathered in the oak, maple, and birch trees on our property before they headed south for the winter. Their cacophonous calls before they flew off were deafening, eerie, and wonderful. In the winter, those that stayed behind pecked at the food my

Humans assign different attributes or symbolism to different birds depending upon the culture. For instance in Egypt, the crane is about vigilance. In China, it represents happiness and a long life. The crane was sacred to the Celts who called upon it to travel to the spirit world.

father left out for them on the bird tray he built against the kitchen window so we could watch the birds from inside. We knew it was spring once the robins began showing up on our lawn, and the woods were once again filled with bird songs. In the summer, at dusk, I called back and forth with the bob-whites I never saw, "Who-who-white. Who-who-white."

I had favorite birds, of course. I thought the Red-winged Blackbirds were my buddies. I loved watching them at the edge of the marsh, perched on cattails, the red patch on their black wings popping with vibrancy as they called out. I was certain these birds knew me just as I knew them.

I was also fond of hawks. I would watch them circling above and wave to them. I knew they liked meat, so I used to leave pieces of chicken or beef out in a snag close to the marsh. The offerings always disappeared, and I was thrilled the hawks took the meat—although really, I think I knew that's probably not what happened.

When I look back at it now, I suppose those big black circling birds may have been vultures rather than hawks. We didn't have bird books, google, or any bird identifying apps—we didn't have any apps, phones that answered questions, or computers! I probably pointed to the sky once and asked my dad what the big black circling bird was and he told me it was a hawk. My dad was rarely wrong, especially about Nature, so they probably were hawks.

Cardinals, blue jays, crows, Orioles, sparrows, starlings, hummingbirds, and pheasants also lived on our property or in the vicinity as well as other birds whose names I didn't know.

One hot summer night after everyone was asleep except me, I thought I heard someone scream outside. I was certain someone was getting killed. I ran into my father's room and shook him awake. "Dad! Someone is screaming!" He padded to the front door in his boxers, T-shirt, and bare feet. He stood behind the screen door—I can still see him in my mind's eye—with the deep darkness of a humid summer night beyond him as he listened. He heard the sound. I must have heard it, too, but I don't remember it the second time. He turned around and padded back to the bedroom as he mumbled, "It's a screech owl."

"Why is it screaming?" I asked.

"To scare prey out into the open so it can see them."

I think he fell back asleep before he reached the bed.

I never saw an owl growing up, but I still haven't forgotten that night half a century later.

Our rural elementary school was surrounded by fields on three sides. Killdeer liked to nest there on the ground. One year, a bunch of boys decided it would be fun to destroy the eggs in the killdeer nests. I don't know why. Maybe they liked watching the way the killdeer would pretend to be injured in an attempt to lure the boys away from the nests, flapping one wing like it was broken. I decided I was going to save the birds. So every recess for a while I would run into the fields after the boys, fighting with them in an attempt to defend the nests.

Cactus Wren

It was awful. I was tiny, and I don't think my flailing arms and legs did much to stop them, but I tried. It was so upsetting that at some point I thought I had a bird fetus on my sweater—because the boys would smash and fling the eggs—and I went screaming back to the school, begging someone to get the dead baby bird off of me. There was no baby bird; I was so traumatized by the brutality of the boys and my inability to stop them that I had hallucinated.

Many years later, as an adult, I began volunteering as a steward at the Steigerwald Lake National Refuge in Washougal, Washington. Every other person I met was a birder. I didn't consider myself a birder. I just liked being out in Nature, and I loved watching birds. I soaked up whatever information I could from the people I met along the trail. I spent hours watching bald eagles, Great Blue Herons, pileated woodpeckers, and kingfishers.

At that time, I lived in the Columbia River Gorge, so I got to observe ospreys and bald eagles almost every day,

People have been feeding birds for thousands of years. Ancient Hindus began the practice of *bhutayajna* which was the feeding of wild animals, including birds. The African Sacred Ibis and Peregrine Falcon were sacred to the ancient Egyptians. They set aside land to feed these birds. In 1825, British poet and naturalist John Freeman Milward Dovaston invented what he called the Ornithotrophe, a kind of hanging bird feeder.

along with stellar jays, flickers, and other birds. I did not become an expert by any means, but I did enjoy watching.

Eventually my husband, Mario Milosevic, and I moved to Arizona onto 4.4 acres in the foothills of the foothills of the Rincon Mountains, a mile from the Saguaro National Park East. We began observing birds we had not seen in decades (since leaving the Midwest)—like Northern Cardinals—along with birds we hadn't known before, especially after we put out water stations for the animals—like Phainopepla and Pyrrhuloxia.

We started driving to places just to see birds, especially when the pandemic was in full swing and we couldn't go indoors anywhere. We would meet people on the trail who would ask, eagerly, "Are you birders?" And we'd say, "No, we just like watching birds." We still figured a birder would know a lot about birds, and we didn't. As time went on, we realized that a birder could just be a bird watcher and a bird lover, and we were certainly that.

Not everyone understands this interest.

For instance when Mario told his mother we were going out to look for birds, she said, "Birds? Why are you looking for birds? You mean like birds you see in your yard?"

"Yeah. We like to find them, listen to them, watch them."

"*Birds*?" Incredulous.

"Yes, birds."

That's all right. People have different interests. And as my mother used to say, "Whatever floats your boat." Watching birds floats my boat. And I hope my boat floats right by a spoonbill or a green heron or maybe a flock of flamingoes.

You Do You Doing the Bird Hour

If you want to try the Bird Hour, go for it. There are no rules except the rule that no one talks about the Bird Hour. Just kidding. I've already told you our rules, but here they are again: No thinking or talking about anything except birds for an hour. We can use a bird identification app on our phones (like Merlin from the Cornell Lab of Ornithology) as long as it works on airplane mode.

When *you* do the Bird Hour, you can sit. You can walk. Try to be outdoors in Nature if you can. If you're indoors, you might want to open your window to listen to the birds. Set a timer if you need to so that you don't (metaphorically) wander away from only birds for the hour. After a while, you won't need the timer.

What if you don't have time for an hour of birds? Don't stress yourself. You get to decide. Try an hour. If you absolutely can't do an hour, try 30 minutes, 15, ten, whatever. Or split the time over the course of the day. If an hour doesn't seem manageable, try ten minutes and work up to an hour. Do a few minutes on your lunch break or first thing in the morning. You get to decide. Don't turn it into something you "have to do." The purpose is to help calm you and to nurture and nourish you with Nature. I hope it is something you will look forward to doing.

Northern Cardinal

It is often instructive to go to the same place again and again to observe birds, especially if it's your own backyard. Go at the same time of day for a while and see what you notice. Then go to the same place at different times of the day. What is different? What is the same?

Be still. I don't mean you have to be frozen still, but you can sit for a time and see what happens. After a while, the birds might take you for part of the scenery or at least realize you aren't a predator in this situation.

Mario was sitting outside reading the other day and didn't notice the Cooper's Hawk in the bird bath just feet away from him. It could be the hawk didn't notice him because Mario was so still—or at least figured he wasn't a threat. Both looked up at me when I stepped outside, and the bird flew away.

And you can turn the Bird Hour into the plant hour or the wild horse hour or whatever else in nature calls to you. I enjoy birds, but I would have loved to spend an hour with bobcats every day. The problem is that the bobcats who live on our property (or nearby) don't turn up often. Same with the coyotes, badgers, rabbits, and javelinas who live here. Birds are always around. Almost wherever you are, you will find birds.

In a nutshell it's very simple: Just sit with the birds. Think about nothing except birds, or think of nothing at all. Just be with the birds. Walk with the birds if you like. You don't need to know anything about birds. Or you can know a lot about birds. Let any expectations go. Just be with the birds. For an hour. That's how you do the Bird Hour.

What Equipment Do You Need for the Bird Hour?

As I mentioned earlier, you only need yourself. However, if you want to identify bird sounds by using an app on your phone, go ahead and bring your phone. Use an app that works on airplane mode. You don't want to be disturbed by texts or phone calls during the Bird Hour. A pair of binoculars can enhance your viewing. Maybe sketching helps you relax and focus, so bring a sketchpad. I am a photographer. I almost always bring my camera, but the purpose of the hour isn't for me to get a great shot. My purpose is to be with the birds.

Can I Include Family and Friends in My Bird Hour or Go It Alone?

Whether you go alone or include others in your Bird Hour is up to you. Why are you doing Bird Hour? If it is to get time alone in Nature, then go alone. If it is to focus on one thing instead of a million things, consider letting others accompany you. Make certain they understand the purpose: No talking about anything but birds. If you have kids with

Flycatcher and Cardinal

you, you might have to emphasize no phones (except for an ID app). You could always try it with your children and partner and see how they like it. It can be a great way to bond and to learn from each other about birds!

You can even make the Bird Hour into a family outing where you go to places where you're likely to encounter more birds. You can have a family list of birds seen or heard or you can each have lists to compare and contrast.

Leave your dogs at home. Birds see dogs as predators, and they will most often fly away in the presence of dogs.

Do what isn't stressful. It's best if the Bird Hour is relaxing for you—and fun is always a bonus.

What If the Weather is Bad?

Remember, it's up to you when and how you do the Bird Hour. If you can't go outside for whatever reason, see if there's a window in your place that gives you a view of birds. This will most likely happen if there's a tree nearby, a water station (like a bird bath), or a bird feeder. If none of these exist where you are, you can always provide water or seed for the birds within a view of a window. Just remember to clean the water stations and feeders. Be aware if you put out feeders the seeds can attract other animals besides birds. Planting trees, bushes, and

Research indicates humans started using birds as food at least 3,500 years ago and maybe up to 10,000 years ago.

other plants for birds might be a better choice.

Even when the weather might not be ideal, it can be fun to bird watch. Once we were wandering around our small town in Washington state after a snowstorm, and we came upon about 50 American Robins perched in a tree, looking like living ornaments on the snow-covered branches. It was one of the more arresting and beautiful things I've seen in my life.

You never know what you'll find when you're out wandering.

The Bird Hour Journal

As I mentioned earlier, I wrote about our Bird Hours when we first started. I've included some of those journal entries in the next few pages to give you an idea about how our hours went. All of them are in May and June when there are many birds out and about in southeast Arizona. Perhaps these entries will inspire your Bird Hour or give you ideas about what you don't want to do!

Elegant Trogon

We live on 4.4 acres in the Sonoran Desert at a place we call the Sanctuary, named after the setting of my novel *Church of the Old Mermaids*. Mario and I came here for writing retreats every winter for more than a decade before the owners sold the place. Several years later it same up for sale again, and we were able to purchase it. Many of the Bird Hours I documented were spent on the Sanctuary.

After a while, I stopped writing about the Bird Hour and just enjoyed the time without feeling as though I needed to record it. However, if you do the Bird Hour, make it your own. You might want to keep a record of the birds you observe. It's all up to you. I try not to do anything with this process that will cause any stress or any need to *do* more. Instead, I want to *be* with the birds. Sometimes that means I write about it; sometimes that means I don't.

May 16, 10:44 a.m. Casita Porch

I've decided to sit for an hour each day with the birds. It'll be one hour a day where I can concentrate on one thing, where I can leave behind anxiety, depression, and despair about the state of the world. At least, that is my hope.

I've chosen birds for a number of reasons. First we have a lot of birds on the Sanctuary. I hear and see them all day long (if I'm outside or looking outside). Sometimes I am awakened mid-night or early morning by the sound of a Great Horned Owl calling out in our pine tree. During the quail love season, we hear the plaintive calls of more than one male Gambel's Quail: over and over and over. (And I mutter, "She's just not into you, dude. Move on.")

For another reason, birds communicate, almost constantly. I feel as though I've spent most of my life around people who don't communicate or don't communicate well. Or I'm being criticized for the way I communicate: I answer emails too quickly or I'm too direct or I'm rude. Something. From my perspective, people are constantly withholding communication, as a way to punish or manipulate or force change. But birds, nah. Nothing like that. They are communicating all the time. They're talking to each other, of course, not to me, but if I pay attention, I can sometimes figure out what's going on in their world. And their world is part of my world.

Scientific research tells us that birdwatching is good for our health. Being out in Nature can improve our sense of well-being, and bird-watching and bird-listening can reduce our stress and help improve our mental and physical health. Plus, it's just fun!

When the birds make sense to me, the world makes sense for a while.

I love wildlife. We have bobcats on our land. I would sit with them for an hour and have the Bobcat Hour if I could. Or 24 hours. Or every day. But I don't see them every day. In fact, I don't see them often. The only wildlife I can observe with some regularity are birds. Birds and ants. I've decided I'd prefer to sit with birds.

I'm not what birders would call a "birder." Expert birders would most likely laugh at me. I'm not good at noticing differences in birds that look a lot alike—which is important when birding. For instance, I just discovered four years after living here that we have two different thrashers on our land: a Curve-billed Thrasher and a Bendire's Thrasher. The Bendire's Thrasher is smaller than the Curve-billed Thrasher with much less curve in the bill. I had seen them before and noticed some difference, but I assumed the Bendire's was just a younger curve-billed. I mention this because I think it means I'm never gonna be an expert on birds. I can only tell you that I enjoy being in their company.

This first Bird Hour, I sat on a lounge chair on the Casita porch that faces the Casita Garden. The Casita is attached to our house, but it is a small apartment that we rent out. Mario and I spent ten winters in it before we bought the place. Right now the Casita is empty. So I sat on the shady porch facing the mesquite tree at the center of the Casita garden and looked out at the bird bath/water station and the plants around the garden.

Ash-throated Flycatcher

The chimes moved gently in the breeze. As I listened, I remembered getting the chimes at New Renaissance Bookstore in Portland. I suddenly felt such a longing for my old home in the Columbia River Gorge. Then the anxiety began to rise. I breathed deeply. One of our recent guests told us they loved the chimes so much that they were going to order the same ones. This memory made me smile. The anxiety lessened.

A female house finch flew into the tree just then. She looked around and then ducked down to the bird bath, took a couple of sips and flew away. I leaned back in the chaise lounge. Eventually a Pyrrhuloxia—the Desert Cardinal—flew into the mesquite tree for a few minutes, followed by a thrasher, and more finches.

The chimes moved. I could hear the buzz of many insects flying around me. Three times I heard mosquitoes, but I guess I was able to bat them away because I didn't get bitten. In the near distance, doves and quails seemed to take turns calling out. A bright red Northern Cardinal flew by, followed by a Cactus Wren. Cactus Wrens are somewhat large wrens, rather twitchy, brown with spots and a long tail. If you see one, there are usually others nearby. They often descend all at once, three or four of them, reminding me of some kind of bird gang. The song "When you're a Jet, you're a Jet all the way" comes to mind whenever I see them. Today I saw just one.

A white butterfly wandered through the air like a drunken helicopter—if helicopters could be drunk—almost stopping here and there and then here. An orange butterfly flew by at a breakneck speed. Trying to outrun something?

It felt so lovely just sitting on the chaise lounge in this beautiful place. My out-of-control anxiety was gone. I knew it was temporary, this lack of anxiousness, but I didn't dwell on that fact. Right now, it was just me and the birds, no third party anxiety.

Suddenly all was quiet. I had noticed this before when I was out with the birds and on the land. Sometimes this meant a hawk was on the hunt. And just like that, a hawk flew right over my head and into the mesquite tree.

It was a Cooper's Hawk, and it looked right at me as it perched in the mesquite, staring at me with bright red eyes. A moment later, it flew to the water station. I slowly picked up the camera, looked in the viewfinder, and took a few photos of it. Some birds flinch when they hear the sound of my camera. When that happens, I stop taking photos. I took a photo here, and the Cooper's Hawk did not flinch.

Cooper's Hawk (*Accipiter cooperri*): 14-20" up to 3' wingspan. Medium-sized hawk. Long rounded tail at the tip. Non-migrator. Kind of looks like it's wearing a black toupee. Preys on birds, mostly medium-sized birds. The Tucson area has a lot of Cooper's Hawks. According to Tucson Audubon, "In a study of more than 300 Cooper's Hawk skeletons, 23 percent showed old, healed-over fractures in the bones of the chest." Yikes! I guess being a predator ain't always easy.

It didn't seem to care. It looked at me several times. I knew I didn't matter to it: I was not friend or foe.

I liked that.

Cooper's Hawks are on the Sanctuary frequently. They seem to like our water stations. Or they like that other birds like our water stations, so they come here hunting for prey. I've seen a Cooper's Hawk in the mesquite tree disemboweling another bird more than once. Birds eating birds makes me queasy. Cooper's Hawks all have to eat, but it feels like dogs eating dogs or people eating people. It's icky to me.

Of course, I'm not judging; I just can't help that it grosses me out. Yet truth to tell, I often call the Cooper's Hawks the serial killers of the Sanctuary.

This morning, I wasn't thinking about any of this. I was only thinking about how absolutely beautiful this bird is. I loved that it wasn't trying to get away from me. It wasn't judging me—except perhaps judging that I wasn't a threat. It wasn't trying to get me to do anything different, to be anyone different, to change who I am. It was just there with me in this space.

Ahhhh.

Yes.

Yes.

Yes.

This is why I watch birds.

May 17, 1:50 p.m. Kim's Office, Sonoran Desert

The air was too polluted to be outside today, so we went to my office for the Bird Hour. My window faces east and looks out onto the desert and the Rincon Mountains. Close to the window is a tall old palo verde wrapped up with an old sprawling mesquite.

If I don't make a lot of noise or move around a lot, my window is a perfect blind. It's tough to get anything done in my office without the shades closed because the wildlife here is so entertaining.

One winter day, two bobcat babies playing in the palo verde entertained us for a time. Coyotes, javelinas, lizards, rabbits, and any number of birds wander through often.

This afternoon, the first bird we saw was a Gila Woodpecker when it flew into the palo verde. Along with the Gambel's Quail, the Gila Woodpecker is the bird we hear most often on the Sanctuary. I might actually hear the White-winged Doves and Mourning Doves more often, but I tend to let those sounds fade into the background if I can.

The Gila Woodpecker is a noisy bird a little bigger than a robin and a little smaller than a crow. They are brown with black-barred wings. The male has a red spot on the top of his head. They nest in saguaro holes they've made. When they're done with them, other birds use the holes for nests. We've often seen them dipping their beaks into the saguaro flowers. They are part of the web of the Sanctuary and often fly noisily not very high above our heads.

Today, this Gila Woodpecker pecked on the palo verde and then hopped onto the nearby bench and seemed to be feasting on something there. After it flew away, a female came and pecked at the tree, probably eating insects we couldn't see.

It was a slow bird afternoon. Mario and I flipped through bird books and discussed the difference between sapsuckers and wood- peckers. Sapsuckers make holes in trees to get sap to run so that the sap attracts bugs that the sapsuckers then return to eat; woodpeckers are pounding on the trees to find insects.

Black-headed Grosbeak

Thunder rolled through the valley. Storm clouds began to cover the blue sky. We wished for rain and more birds, but it didn't rain and the birds were scarce. And then our hour was up.

May 18, 8:19 a.m. The Barn area: Bobcat House Porch Facing North and Raised Bed Corral Facing South

It was nice to be outside after days of ozone pollution. The rain from the day before had cleared out some of the pollution. The air felt fresh and humid. As I walked to the barn, several rabbits ran in front of me. It was good to see the rabbits coming back to the Sanctuary. They had suffered their own pandemic beginning in 2020. So many had died, but it appeared they were recovering. It was almost Bird Hour. Time to put away worrying about rabbits to be with the birds.

I noticed bird feathers on the loveseat on the Bobcat House porch. The Cooper's Hawk had probably feasted on a little bird here recently. I was glad I had missed it.

Mario joined me this morning again. We sat beside each other on the Bobcat House porch and looked around. Two young palo verde trees near us were bright with yellow flowers. Beyond them in the distance the Catalina Mountains towered over the valley. I heard the sounds of some kind of construction in the near distance. I couldn't see it, but I heard machinery. Fortunately the drone of the bees all around us was louder than the machines. And a Northern Cardinal was perched in a nearby mesquite, tweet-tweet-tweeting.

Gila Woodpecker (*Melanerpes uropygialis*): 9". Medium-sized. The males have a red cap. Non-migrator. Both male and female incubate the young, usually in a saguaro cavity that they excavated the year before. They are noisy! When a hawk is nearby, they will alarm over and over, usually until the hawk leaves. At least that's the case on the Sanctuary.

The sun was shining, the sky was blue. A Curve-billed Thrasher began singing its beautiful love song from its perch at the top of a pencil cholla. White-winged Doves shuffled in the dirt in front of the porch for a bit. A Cactus Wren called out loudly now and again. Two hummingbirds flitted by— not sure what kind.

It was fairly quiet. Mario picked up one of our bird books and began reading it. He mentioned that tanagers had been reclassified as cardinals. Cardinals, grosbeaks, buntings, and tanagers are now in the same family. That is a list of birds I love! I think it's something to do with their beaks. The beaks are bigger than those on other birds, proportionally, at least on the grosbeaks and cardinals. I have a badly broken nose that looks perpetually swollen. Perhaps that is why I adore these birds so much.

Halfway through the Bird Hour, we moved to the other side of the barn. We heard many more birds there, especially fly-catchers. We saw movement in the trees, but we couldn't identify any particular bird. Our bird identification app on our phones said an Indigo Bunting, Black-headed Grosbeak, and Western Tanager were all near, but we didn't see any of them. We heard Western Tanagers over and over, but they were invisible to us. I had this strange sense of FOMA—fear of missing out—for the entire hour. I wanted to see all of these wonderful birds!

And then the hour was over.

Hoping tomorrow I can get that sense of peace back again. The Bird Hour is not a competition, I told myself. It's just a way to be with nature and relax.

May 19, 6:49 a.m. Patagonia, Along Sonoita Creek

We began our Bird Hour walking on a path along the Sonoita Creek in the Patagonia-Sonoita Creek Preserve. We immediately startled a Great Blue Heron that we hadn't seen before it flew up and away. We continued on the path, surrounded by huge old Fremont cottonwoods. I could be with these amazing giants all the days of my life. The birds love them too.

We heard one species after another calling out, including a Gray Hawk, a small hawk that lives in the Patagonia area. We hardly ever see them close up. Mostly they are tiny dots circling in the empty sky. This morning was no different.

The creek curved, the path curved, and we curved. A Great Blue Heron flew up to a snag and landed on top of it. Hardly anything more spectacular looking than an elegant Great Blue Heron perched on a white snag, the sky brilliant blue behind it.

We stood watching the Great Blue Heron for a while. Then suddenly a Gray Hawk came out of the blue and dove at the Great Blue Heron. The heron kept its balance, but it flapped its wings and squawked loudly and continuously for a bit. The Gray Hawk flew away to a cottonwood not far from the heron. They could see each other; that's how

Black Phoebe

near they were to one another. The heron continued to change its posture and give its raspy call. It stretched its neck up until it looked almost giraffe-like while flapping its wings a bit.

Mario and I looked from one bird to another and back again. We were shocked and thrilled. We had spent many hours observing Great Blue Herons over the years when we lived in Washington state and recently after finding a heronry on the San Pedro River. We had never seen another bird come anywhere near a Great Blue Heron let alone attack one.

Gray Hawks are small. The Great Blue Heron is about four times as large as the little hawk. Gray Hawks primarily eat lizards, but they'll eat other small animals, including birds. We had spotted a large nest not far from where the Great Blue Heron was now perched, up in the crotch of an old cottonwood along the river. I had taken photos of it but could not tell what kind of bird was inside, although the beak looked like a hawk's beak. Perhaps the Gray Hawk was protecting the nest?

The two birds stayed in their respective places and gave each other the stink eye (and ignored one another now and again) for a long while. Eventually the Gray Hawk flew somewhere out of our sight although it could have stayed close and we just couldn't see it.

Finally we had gotten to see a Gray Hawk up close and in person! And any day with a Great Blue Heron is a good day.

Our hour was up, but we kept hiking, watching, and listening for a couple more hours.

Birds chattered all around us. Once I heard about four different calls so I stood in front of a small bushy riparian tree where the sound was coming from. I looked and looked, and I could not see any birds! It made me laugh. What a great talent: to be noisy and yet invisible to harm.

We came to a place in the path where we often see ravens. Sure enough a couple of ravens began flying around a huge old cottonwood. We looked up into the tree and saw a flat round nest high up but below most of the canopy. Inside the nest, we could see at least two big red gaping mouths. Had we found a raven's nest? We didn't know for certain.

Purple Martin

We would have to come back soon and check on it for sure.

May 20, 8:00 a.m. Pool Patio on the Sanctuary

Ahhhh.

We had lots of things to do today, but we decided to stop everything and have our Bird Hour.

The air was clear, the sky was blue, and we got comfy in our matching chaise lounges, Mario with his binoculars, me with my camera. Between us on a small table were several bird books. We both turned on our bird identification apps.

It was a beautiful morning, and I was grateful for this time and place and the company. The sound of bees came from everywhere. One of our neighbors was using a chainsaw—or something like it—but they didn't use it the entire hour and after a while, I didn't notice it.

Lots of birds showed up. We could see motion in the desert hackberry on the other side of the wall. The thorny tree is covered in tiny black berries right now, and the birds love them.

A male Phainopepla showed up right away. He kept himself mostly hidden in the hackberry, but every once in a while I could see his shiny black coat or red eyes through the green.

Several Curve-billed Thrashers took turns hopping onto our lowest water station, but they never took a drink. Several others moved back and forth in the hackberry, scarfing down berries.

We have lots of Curve-billed Thrashers on the Sanctuary. Their irritated-sounding "wheet-wheet" call is very familiar. They perch near the top of a bush or tree and sing a beautiful song, too. Apparently they mate for life. Mario read from one of our books, "They drive out Cactus Wrens from their territory."

I didn't like hearing that. I love Cactus Wrens. We consider them de facto mascots of the Sanctuary. They seem so mischievous and full of energy.

Curve-billed Thrashers not only drive out Cactus Wrens, Mario told me, they destroy their nests.

I had an urge to get up and chase the thrashers away from our hackberry bushes. I didn't do it.

Mario said, "I like them. Thrashers have a lot of personality."

He's right. The thrashers bee-bop around the Sanctuary, digging furiously in the dirt with their long curved bills, searching for

Northern Cardinal (*Cardinalis cardinalis*): Non-migrator. The male is bright red with a black mask and a red bill. The female is buff brown with a black mask and red bill. During courtship, the male feeds the female. Both males and females sing. Very territorial in the spring. Females incubate the eggs. After hatching, the male will feed the babies, often while the female is off building another nest for their second brood.

food and leaving behind hole after hole after hole as they move along.

During our Bird Hour today, we kept hearing a kind of clicking sound. We thought maybe a bird was cracking something open. But we didn't know. It went on most of the hour. I went to the palm tree and looked up. A female Hooded Oriole was inside one of the nests they had built a couple of years ago. That was where the clicking sounds were coming from. It looked like she was weaving more things into the nest. As far as we knew, the nests (two of them) were never used. That year we saw several females around the Sanctuary but no males, and the nests were unused. This year, the Sanctuary has at least

Great Blue Heron

two males. Maybe the nests will have some nestlings this year!

I love when we have nests on the Sanctuary. I'm saddened that so many don't make it. We've had doves built nests on our porch twice this season, and they've dropped the eggs on the cement twice. No babies.

A year or two ago, a Curve-billed Thrasher built a nest in pencil cholla along the path going into the Big Corral (it's a big field). We saw three beautiful blue eggs. And then one day they were gone. A predator must have gotten them. The nest is still there. It was rebuilt and refreshed this year, but we haven't seen any birds around it and no eggs inside.

We had a Vermillion Flycatcher pair build a nest in the palo verde right outside my office window. I was thrilled to watch them build the nest, sit on it, tend to it, and then one day, they just went away. I don't know if she never laid any eggs or if the eggs just never hatched. I haven't seen them since.

However, we saw nestlings in a roadrunner nest twice. And we've seen many haggard adult birds trying to feed fledglings. So we know lots of nests here must make good homes. I hope the Orioles have babies that survive.

The bird identification app said we had an Indigo Bunting in the area. We looked around excitedly. I had seen a female Indigo Bunting outside my window in the palo verde earlier in the week. I would love to see the gorgeous blue male. But we didn't see either male or female this morning.

A tiny Lucy's Warbler showed up at our lowest water station. They appear to be so delicate. I hope they're not. One needs to be tough to survive the desert.

May 21, 6:30 a.m. Hummingbird Corner on the Sanctuary in the Sonoran Desert

For the Bird Hour this morning, we chose an area outside our wall on the south side of the house. We sat with a mesquite and palo verde behind us. Before us was a sweet acacia and eucalyptus tree. We could see the pine tree, too. We sat and listened and prepared to be dazzled.

I was exhausted. I had barely slept the night before, and I was grumpy as hell. But no matter how tired I was I couldn't sit there during the Bird Hour thinking about how tired I was. That would defeat the purpose of the Bird Hour.

Northern Harrier

I tried to redirect my thoughts.

We call this spot in the Sanctuary hummingbird corner because a hummingbird almost always shows up when we come to this area. We figured there must be a nest or two nearby although we've never seen one.

Almost as soon as we sat down, a female broad-billed hummingbird whizzed by us and flitted back and forth from branch to branch in the eucalyptus tree right in front of us. A male traded places with her for a bit. Several other hummingbirds came by, but they were so fast, we couldn't tell what kind they were.

A Verdin flew up to the top of the pine tree and looked spectacular in the early morning sunlight. Mario read aloud about Verdins from one of our field guides: Apparently the male builds several nests, then shows them to the female; she picks the one she prefers, and that's where they raise a family. The fledglings actually come back to the nest after they've left it, which is unusual for birds.

I like Verdins. They are easy to identify—pale yellow head and a small red patch on their shoulders—and they visit our water stations frequently. They don't seem as skittish around us as most of the other birds are.

We heard many birds for this Bird Hour, some we could identify, some we couldn't. I was so tired that my mind kept wandering. I wanted the hummingbirds to move slower so I could see them or photograph them. I felt grumpy about everything. And then one of the hummingbirds perched on a pencil cholla snag not far from us. As I watched it, I sighed and leaned back in my chair. It didn't matter that I was exhausted. It didn't matter how fast the birds moved. It did not matter if I didn't see another bird the whole hour. It was enough to sit here in the shade under a blue blue sky with my sweetheart and watch a tiny hummingbird take in the world.

It was enough.

May 22, 6:30 a.m. Along the San Pedro River in the San Pedro Riparian National Conservation Area

To drop down into this riparian area with the tall Fremont cottonwoods shading the river and us is like stepping into heaven. The river runs beside us, muddy now, slow and mysterious, and all around birds are calling out, nearly shouting to be noticed, but probably not by us.

I feel such a profound happiness when I am here.

And now that the Bird Hour has begun, I don't think about how much danger the river is in, and I don't think about the cattle that were recently trampling the river banks and everything around it. Nope, I am trying to quell my almost constant panic about the state of the world, my nearly constant anxiety about Mario and anyone I love, including myself. The Bird Hour is about one thing: *birds*.

Great Blue Heron (*Ardea herodias*): 42-52". Non-migrator in Arizona. Biggest heron in North America. Mostly feeds while standing in water. Nests in colonies. Both parents incubate the eggs and feed the young. When humans get too close, the great blue will call out and then fly away. The call sounds very cranky, so we have nicknamed it the "big cranky."

We are both listening and glancing at our phones to see what the bird ID app is picking up. I find this helps teach me what certain birds sound like. Our bird ID app doesn't always get it right, of course, but it gets it more right than we do.

The grass and other vegetation had gotten a lot higher in just the last week. In some places along the path, the grass came up to my waist. I checked for ticks each time we

went through a tall patch and then continued looking for birds.

We stopped at the heronry to see how
the nestlings were doing. We had found the
nests a few months ago. Every week we
watched the adults building the nests and
then sitting in the nests and now we had
seen babies for the last two or three weeks.
This was a small heronry with only three
nests and one wasn't in use. The one on our
left had had two nestlings in it. Today we
only saw one. Had one already fledged? Or
had it died? One had definitely been smaller
than the other. We could see movement in
the second nest, but we couldn't tell how
many babies were in it.

After a while, we left the herons and
hiked to the lake. The Red-winged Blackbirds called out again and again. We were
hoping to see the Least Bittern which we had
spotted last week. Least Bitterns are small
herons. All bitterns are usually difficult to

spot because they blend in so well with the surrounding vegetation and are very still.

When I volunteered as a steward at Steigerwald Refuge in Washougal, Washington, I would sometimes see an American Bittern, which is a medium-sized heron and much bigger than the Least Heron. But this was only after I had been on the refuge for months—maybe even years—and I had learned how to spot the American Bittern in the tall golden marsh grass.

We had seen the Least Bittern by chance here, by the lake, when we accidentally flushed it from the reeds as we walked along the path the week before. It had stood in the middle of the lake for a time, looking regal and colorful and absolutely spectacular— and my camera would not take a photo because it kept focusing on the reeds instead of the bird. I wasn't tall enough to get a photo above the reeds. Ah well. I had seen it, and it was lovely.

Today we didn't find the Least Bittern. I walked along the path away from the lake, and suddenly an owl flew out from one of the trees I had just walked under. It looked white. I watched it fly up into one of the old Fremont cottonwoods closer to the river. It turned to face me, and I saw it was a Barn Owl! I had never seen a Barn Owl before in real life.

The Least Bittern was forgotten. I called to Mario, and we hurried down the path toward the river as we looked up and tried to follow the errant Barn Owl.

What is it about owls? I grew up in the country, and I don't remember ever

Anna's Hummingbird

seeing an owl. At the Sanctuary, a Great Horned Owl (sometimes with a companion) visits us several times a year. We also had two visits—one in the barn and one in the pool patio—of two different kinds of owls, both of them tiny. When an owl is on the Sanctuary, it feels more like home than any other time.

Now, seeing this Barn Owl felt like a gift.

Eventually the Barn Owl flew away into the forest again, and we didn't follow. It was enough to have seen it. Our Bird Hour had become three hours. It was time to head back before it got too hot. But wow: a Barn Owl! It felt mythic, seeing it. Yes, that was it. Every time I saw or heard an owl, I felt like the world I had believed in as a child still existed: a world filled with animals, magic, fairies, and mystery.

Or something. It was just . . . beautiful. Absolutely beautiful.

May 23, 5:49 a.m. On the Sanctuary, Next to the Toolshed

I made sure all the water stations were clean and filled with water, and I watered our potted plants with rain water. Then we sat in chairs by the tool shed in Mario's work area. I wanted to call it "birder's corner," but I changed my mind when the hour was up.

We were in the shade and nearly surrounded by trees. We thought we would see a million birds. In the Rabbit Corrals (the old horse corrals) behind us, we could just see several Gambel's Quail running back and forth. A small bird that looked like a Lucy's Warbler flew into a nearby palo verde tree. Every time it sang, our bird identification app said it was a Nashville Warbler. We thought that was cool since we had never seen one before, but I was pretty certain it was a Lucy's Warbler. (It's just an indication that as wonderful as bird identification apps are, they aren't always right.)

It was a beautiful day: blue sky, slightly cool. It was great sitting outside with Mario. We heard a lot of birds, but we didn't see many. I continued to get glimpses of the quail and I thought I saw an Ash-throated Flycatcher. At one point, we heard what sounded like a Mallard. We thought this was odd, but the bird ID app thought that's what it was, too. Agua Caliente Park is just a few miles from us. Perhaps one of them got lost?

The hour went by quickly and uneventfully. And we went on with our day.

May 24, 6:40 a.m. Patagonia, Arizona, Along Sonoita Creek

We decided we wanted to check out the raven nest we had found on Sunday in Patagonia this morning. It was lovely to be up before the sun and hear all the birds on the Sanctuary. In particular, I heard lots of flycatchers. Early birds, eh?

An hour or so later, we were walking on a path along Sonoita Creek. It was so chilly that we decided against sitting in one spot for our Bird Hour. We followed the path which followed the curve of the river through the old cottonwoods. We heard Yellow-Breasted Chats, yellowthroats, flycatchers, Summer Tanagers, and other birds we didn't recognize.

I was feeling particularly anxious this morning. I get fixated on something that is worrying me, and I have a problem letting it go. I think the stressors from the last few years (particularly the pandemic and the rise of fascism and white supremacy in our country) has dug trenches in my brain, anxiety and fixation ruts that I now easily fall into where I stay trapped. Lately I've been whispering, "Birds, birds, birds," whenever the anxiety threatens to take over. And then I try to think about birds to distract myself. It usually works, except this morning when it wasn't.

Lightning Bird

Mario stopped to gaze across a huge open field where we often see Wild Turkeys and various flycatchers. I kept going. It was chilly this morning, and I wanted to warm up. Looking through my camera lens, I gazed at the top of one of the old cotton-woods where I thought I had seen a bird. As I looked away, I spotted a big brown some-thing in the near distance in the trees along the path. I figured it was probably a vulture. But I stopped and looked more carefully.

It was not a vulture.

It was an owl.

No. It was one

two

three owls. Owlets maybe?

They seemed to be huddled together about 20 feet up, and they were watching me. They had eyes like a Great Horned Owl, but they didn't have any horns. Too young?

I was so excited I could barely move or breathe. I didn't want to do anything to scare them. I turned around and saw Mario coming toward me. I whispered loudly and motioned for him to come closer.

And then we were side by side under a clear blue sky in the morning light gazing at three young owls who were gazing at us. They looked small, but the male Great Horned Owl is small, so we didn't know if we were seeing two or three owlets (or if one was an adult).

It didn't matter. We just wanted to spend the day with them. Or forever with them. We watched them watch us. We watched them close their eyes and sleep a bit but mostly they watched us.

I have always said when the Great Horned Owl is at the Sanctuary, we feel more at home. Now I was seeing *three* Great Horned Owls. Was this home for me? Was this the Universe's way of saying this was home? (Not that I thought the Universe really had time to plan my life.) We did love this area, but they were building a mine just a few miles down the road. Thousands of people would soon be moving here, and the mine could contaminate the watershed. They would be dumping tens of thousands of gallons of used water into the creek every day.

We could not move here.

Watching the owls perched together, all three of them, I thought of the three faces of the goddess: maiden,

Black-throated Sparrow

mother, and crone. Even though other cultures associate owls with various goddesses, I most often think of Athene/Athena, who was an ancient Minoan Goddess (long before the Greeks got her). She represents healing, alchemy, self-hood. In my MommaEarth Goddess Runes that I created 30 years ago this month, I wrote that Athene "will help you to stand firm in yourself and be an alchemist: changing lead to gold in all aspects of your life. Call upon her to help in healing and transformations of all kinds."

Great Horned Owlets

Of course these owlets were their own selves. They weren't put here for me to have an epiphany. Or to feel better. Or anything to do with me. Yet I felt filled up with wonder and joy.

We stayed a long while with the owls/owlets. Then we kept going on the path to look for the raven nest. At first, we couldn't find it. And just about the time we were going to head back, we heard the baby ravens fussing. Mario got a different perspective on the tree we were under, and he found the nest again. There they were!

With their huge gaping mouths. An adult was in the nest with them this time. A Gray Hawk dive-bombed the nest, but no one was hurt, and the hawk flew on.

On the way back, we stopped by the tree where the owlets were perched. We were thrilled they were still there. If these three were all fledglings, then I suspected at least one parent would have to be close by. I casually looked around. Not far from the owlet tree, I saw an adult Great Horned Owl perched and sleeping—probably exhausted from feeding her/his children. I don't know why, but I felt better knowing a parent was close. We said goodbye to the babies and headed down the path away from the owls.

What a spectacular day. Never in my life had I seen *four* owls.

Best day ever.

May 25, 6:30 a.m. Patagonia, Along Sonoita Creek

We don't usually wander far from home two days in a row. For one thing, gas prices in the Tucson area right now are at least a dollar higher than anywhere else in the U.S. For another thing, we like being on the Sanctuary. But the company Mario had been working with for the last couple of years was going belly-up. It was a job Mario loved, and it was difficult to see it all go away. When he was home, he was mostly on the computer talking with other people in the company or on zoom calls or texting. He needed a Bird Hour: a time where all we did was think about, watch, and listen to birds. So we decided to return to Patagonia to see if we could find the owlets again.

Verdin (*Auriparus flaviceps*): 4.5"
Non-migrator. Light gray/brown, rusty-red shoulder patch (often hidden), yellow head. It is not closely related to any other bird in the Western Hemisphere! Female incubates the eggs. Both momma and poppa feed the young. According to Richard Cachor Taylor, "The distribution of Verdins in Arizona is almost identical to the range of Arizona's mesquite."

On the way there, we talked about how to make a living now so we could keep the Sanctuary and just . . . live. Everything has gotten so expensive—especially food—that any loss of income was noticed. I said, "It's time I get back to writing. So let's come up with a novel idea for me." Mario laughed. Just like that I was gonna come up with an idea? But I started talking, and an idea, characters, and plot just flowed out of me, as if it had been waiting for me to say yes—like the old days when I was writing fiction all the time. It even had a birding angle. We batted around a title (because I can't start a book

without a title). By the time we got to Patagonia, I had the skeleton of the novel—and a
title. Perhaps the Bird Hour was doing ex-
actly what I had hoped: helping to change
my brain by giving it and my nervous system
a rest from the constant barrage of horrible
news and anxiety. Yes!

This morning we didn't stop at the Paton
Center for Hummingbirds. Instead we went
straight to the trail along the creek. It was
cool out, and sweet light filtered down
through the old cottonwoods along the path.
The creek gurgled pleasantly beside us. We
could hear the almost constant tttttt of a Yellow-Breasted Chat somewhere in the woods,
along with many bird calls and songs we
didn't recognize. I kept thinking I heard an
American Robin, but it turned out to be a
Summer Tanager, I believe. It was a lovely
song.

We quickly reached the tree where the
owlets had been the day before. They were

gone. We looked for the parent, too. We found a long old owl feather (and left it) but no owls.

Ah well. Seeing four owls in one day had been somewhat of a miracle. We couldn't expect to repeat it. It was a beautiful clear blue morning now. We could hear lots of birds. So we continued on the trail. We went to the raven nest. Today the nestlings looked more like ravens than they had yesterday, darker, as if they were getting feathers. Not sure how it's possible to change that much in 24 hours, but that was my observation.

We met a couple near the raven nest. They asked us if we had any lifers today. That took me a second, and then I remembered that was a birding term for a first time sighting. I told them we hadn't and asked them if they had seen anything this morning. The man told us it was their first time on this trail. Yesterday they had been up at Madera Canyon for the first time, and they had seen

an Elegant Trogon. I gasped. Their first time!
Within minutes of arriving! They had seen
the bird that some people search an entire
lifetime for? Yep. I congratulated them. We
had seen the Elegant Trogon once, and that
had been a day to remember. I was secretly
envious, but I was also very glad for them. I
understood what a thrill
it was to see this beautiful, rare, and colorful
bird.

Great Horned Owl

Mario and I stopped
by the Henry Moore
downed tree. (It looks
like a Henry Moore
sculpture: this huge old
dead cottonwood, its
trunk bare, gray-white, and shiny, sprawled
across the forest floor.) Mario sat on the
bench there while I wandered in the area. I
spotted a hummingbird flying around a
sapling just off the trail. Then she stopped

and just stayed there, on the branch that was about four feet off the ground. I squinted. She was sitting on something. I lifted up my camera to get a better look. She was sitting on a tiny perfect nest! It reminded me of half of a walnut shell. It looked so tidy and expertly made.

I caught Mario's eye and waved him over and showed him my find. We were both in awe. When the hummingbird flew away, I took a quick photo with my phone and hurried back onto the trail. She came back a few minutes later and took her place on the nest again. All was well. It was one of the coolest things I've ever seen. We were both so tickled by the experience.

Wow, wow, wow!

Our Bird Hour lasted for three hours, and we were both happy, happy, happy.

I am loving the Bird Hour.

May 26, 6:19 a.m. Madera Canyon, Arizona

After hearing from the couple on the trail in Patagonia about the Elegant Trogon in Madera Canyon, we decided to head out there Friday morning. We used to visit the canyon about once a week, but during the worst days of the pandemic, people behaved badly. Many brought their dogs off-leash (which was against the rules and the law). We had too many scary confrontations with owners after their dogs came after us, and the place began to feel overrun and unsafe.

But for a long time, it had been one of our favorite places. It was there we first saw the Lightning Bird—or the Yellow-eyed Junco. The story goes that the Indigenous people in Veracruz, Mexico called the Yel-low-eyed Junco the Lightning Bird because the bird gathered sunlight during the day and then released it at night. (Thus the color of its eyes.) I love a good story, and the Lightning Bird story made me love this bird even more! Unfortunately, we have not seen it for a couple of years at least.

Hooded Merganser

This was also the first place we saw Acorn Woodpeckers and alligator junipers. And one amazing June day two years ago, we had an experience with an Elegant Trogon.

It was around 8:00 a.m. which meant it was getting late—for summer in Arizona. We weren't far from the outdoor amphitheater on the path alongside the dry creek. The place seemed deserted.

We were glad no people were around, but where were all the birds? Then I heard this strange almost mechanical sound. I shook my head. Why was someone making that obnoxious noise? It didn't go away, and it didn't change, only now I thought it sounded like a small yappy dog—a small yappy mechanical dog. And then I realized: It was a bird!

"Mario," I whispered. "I think it's a bird. Let's follow it." So we walked around on uneven rocky ground while looking up and trying to follow the sound. I didn't think there was a chance in hell we could find it—whatever it was.

Suddenly I was looking up at a spectacular bird: an Elegant Trogon. It was medium-sized with a long barred black and white tail, a scarlet red belly, a white breast band, and an emerald green head. The eyes were ringed in gold. It didn't fly away. In fact, it seemed to keep us in sight as it hopped from tree to tree, getting lower sometimes which enabled me to take better photos. I had never seen anything like it. How were we lucky enough to find this magnificent bird?

We hung out with it for a long while. At some point it flew off.

Now, this morning, we trudged up a very steep hill/mountain to a place where Elegant Trogons had been spotted many times—and where we had gone before to look for it. I hated this hill. Climbing and especially climbing anything steep and especially climbing anything steep at a higher altitude than I'm used to is problematic because of my asthma. I did not like it.

I encouraged Mario to go on ahead of me. I didn't want him to see me struggling. I said out loud, "Bird Hour, Bird Hour, Bird Hour," trying to get my mind off of how icky I felt. My lungs hurt. My left arm and shoulder hurt. I wondered if I was having a heart attack or if I had just slept on it wrong. Time would tell.

I did not like this freaking hill.

Finally I caught up with Mario. I sat on the bench, legs swinging, and peered around at the tall sycamores, hoping to catch a glimpse of the Elegant Trogon. I had absolutely no expectation that we would find one. My bird identification app was hardly showing any birds at all. If we had stayed home, we would have seen/heard twice as many birds.

Several people went on by us. They either continued up Old Baldy Trail or on to Carrie Nation Trail. None of them seemed to be looking for anything. They were just on their way to somewhere else, I supposed. I picked up my camera and walked around a bit. I heard a strange sound. A

Lucy's Warbler (*Oreothlypis luciae*): 4"
Pearl gray. Migrates to Mexico and Central America. Eye-ring. Rufous crown patch on the male. Smallest warbler in the U.S., only Arizona warbler to nest in cavities. Because of loss of habitat, Lucy's Warblers may be in trouble, so you'll see Lucy's Warblers nest boxes in many places in our area. The female builds the nest. Both parents incubate and feed the young.

barking dog. It was high pitched and obnoxious. Crap, I thought, some asshole was bringing their barking dog up here; we'll never see any birds.

Wait. That wasn't a dog. I glanced at my bird ID app. ELEGANT TROGON.

"Mario! It's an Elegant Trogon."

The faraway call got closer.

And closer.

The sun wasn't up over the mountains yet so the trees were dark. I saw a bird land up high in one of the white sycamores. Its mouth was open, and it was spouting Elegant Trogon sounds.

"It's the Elegant Trogon!" I said to Mario. I pointed and swung up my camera. The bird was black in my viewfinder, but I recognized the shape. I took several photos as it called out.

Two women were coming up the trail. They will be so thrilled the Elegant Trogon is here.

No. They were talking, heads down. They didn't hear the Elegant Trogon. Or they didn't care. They turned up Baldy Trail. The Elegant Trogon had had enough, it seemed. It flew away, still calling out. We listened until we couldn't hear it any longer.

We grinned at each other.

"We came, we saw," Mario said.

I laughed. We had indeed.

We waited around for a little while longer, but we didn't hear or see

Greater Roadrunner

anything. We went to the place where we had seen the Elegant Trogon before. We hoped we might run into the Lightning Bird. We didn't. Acorn Woodpeckers and Mexican Jays entertained us for a bit. A Painted Redstart did some gymnastics before us. Then it got really quiet again. No birds. No people. No animals except some squirrels. We listened to the sound of the creek. It was nice to hear it running so strongly.

After a while, I said to Mario, "The Bird Hour isn't that much fun without birds."

He laughed.

And then we went home.

When we got back to the Sanctuary, ten baby Gambel's Quails and their parents were dipping their beaks into one of our watering stations. A Great Horned Owl watched us from the pine tree. A Hooded Oriole pair was still harvesting nesting material from the palo verde tree. A Gila Woodpecker shouted at us as it flew overhead. Later the bird identification app said a Blue Grosbeak was near. I couldn't find it, but I hoped it was true. Cactus Wrens fed their fledglings while on the Old Mesquite outside my window. A hummingbird flew hither and yon. Mario and I call them the usual suspects. It means I could have the Bird Hour all hours on the Sanctuary.

No Elegant Trogon here, but I like our usual suspects, too.

May 27, 8:45 a.m. Casita Porch, on the Old Mermaids Sanctuary, Sonoran Desert

Mario and I sat in the shade of the Casita porch for the Bird Hour this morning. Almost immediately a male Gambel's Quail began his one note call for love. Over and over and over. He walked along the wall surrounding the Casita Garden and then flew up into the mesquite tree in front of us. And he sang his love call again and again.

Gambel's Quail are usually very skittish birds. We normally cannot get anywhere near them without them squealing and running away. I get my best photos of them from my office window. Momma and Poppa bring their babies there to drink from the water station I've set up near the palo verde tree or to dig around under the trees for goodies. Sometimes the parents fly up into the tree and seem to be teaching babies how to fly. I don't know if they are actually doing that, but that's the story my brain tells me whenever I see them in the tree. They seem like good parents.

Wild Turkey

However, a quick count on the Sanctuary seems to reveal that we have more males than females. This means several males are constantly looking for love. Thus they get onto a fence post or up in a tree and send out their plaintive calls all day long.

This morning, the Gambel's Quail was within feet of us up in the tree. And he just would not stop calling out. It was extremely irritating. "No one wants you, dude," I said. "Please stop."

I got up several times, not so secretly hoping that my presence would send the quail on its way—and we would have some semblance of quiet. But it didn't happen. It stayed in the tree calling out for 45 minutes. It was the first time that the Bird Hour was not relaxing. I tried to think of something else, tried to read about birds in the hopes that I could drown out the sound.

Nope.

When we had just 15 minutes left, we decided to move to the other side of the walled garden so that we wouldn't have to listen to this bird. Mario stood up, and the quail flew away.

Thank goodness!

I love you quails, but Geez Louise, that was obnoxious.

As soon as the quail left, we heard and saw several other birds: finches, Orioles,

Lucy's Warblers, a Mourning Dove, but I was exhausted and ready to go inside and enjoy some silence. So that's what I did as soon as the hour was up.

I guess not every Bird Hour can be a rip-roaring success.

May 28, 8:03 a.m. Pool Patio, on the Old Mermaids Sanctuary, Sonoran Desert

We have two water stations on the Pool Patio, and I expected to see lots of birds there, but maybe it was too late in the day. Or something. We heard the Gambel's Quail—in the distance—among other birds including the Hooded Oriole, House Finch, and Curve-Billed Thrasher. But we did not see many birds. Several Turkey Vultures were riding the thermals over the barn while Mario read aloud from our bird books. The bird identification app picked up the sounds of Purple Martins several times, but we didn't see them. They are such beautiful birds, and their numbers are declining all across the country. Last year I saw many of them in our neighbor's saguaros and out in the park. I haven't seen many this year. It's good to know they are here.

It was a relaxing Bird Hour with the usual suspects.

May 29, 5:30 a.m. Quail House, the Sanctuary, Sonoran Desert

We decided to sit in front of the Quail House for the Bird Hour today. The Quail House is a small studio space for writers on the property out of sight of our house. I've written about a dozen novels in the Quail House; Mario's written about seven. It's a sweet space.

Sitting in front of the Quail House, we are facing east. We are surrounded by creosote, small palo verdes, and pencil cholla. This morning we could hear lots of birds: flycatchers, Phainopepla, Desert Cardinal, Gila Woodpecker, Gambel's Quail, and lots of doves. But once again, we hardly *saw* any birds. I leaned back in my chair and let the bird symphony surround me. Yet as the sun began inching up on the backside of the Rincon Mountains, I wanted to see some birds.

I got up and began to wander. I could hear a male Gambel's Quail again going on and on. He was not getting the love this season. I did not want to listen to it for another hour again. I was glad he flew away once I started walking.

I had found a nest in a tree—not sure what kind of tree it is. The nest was high up, so I couldn't tell if any birds were in it. However, as I neared the tree, I heard the tsk, tsk, tsk of what I thought was a Northern Cardinal. But I soon saw two Pyrrhuloxia—Desert Cardinals—flying around inside the wall of pencil cholla. I didn't know if they were fighting or playing or none of the above. The Pyrrhuloxia isn't as red as the Northern Cardinal and its beak is orange and looks like a parrot beak. They hopped from cholla finger to cholla finger, and then flew off. I soon lost sight of them.

Then I heard a strange almost metal sound which I figured was a Phainopepla on top of a nearby mesquite. They look like small black cardinals. Their name means "shining robe," and they practically live on mistletoe berries. We often see them at the very top of mesquite trees. The male is shiny black and the female is shiny gray. They both have brilliant red eyes. When the male flies, he flashes a white stripe on the underside of his wings. It's always fun to watch. I never tire of seeing them. I know some of their sounds, but they also imitate other birds. I wonder if the bird identification app can tell the difference?

Great Horned Owl (*Bubo virginianus*): 21-25", wingspan up to 4'. Non-migrator. Large owl. Mating pairs are monogamous. Female incubates, both parents feed the young. They usually take over the nest of another large bird. They have an incredibly diverse diet, from scorpions to domestic cats and everything in-between. It will kill skunks and porcupines and is sometimes called the flying tiger.

I continued walking around, this time heading for the barn. I heard a cry and recognized the sound of a Cooper's Hawk. I followed the sound into the Big Corral. I could see what looked like a Cooper's Hawk on the top of a pole. Sharp-shinned Hawks and Cooper's Hawks look like twins to me, but the bird identification app said it was a Cooper's Hawk. Another hawk came and perched next to it. I watched them for a while and then made my way back to Mario by the Quail House.

Verdin

It was good to see the usual suspects out and about this morning.

May 30, 6:14 a.m. Along the San Pedro River

The sky was clear and blue. No wind. The dark green trees growing alongside the river were like beacons of hope in this otherwise sparse brown landscape. We hurried down the path toward the River Trail. The sound of birds came from everywhere even before we reached the river.

Down by the river, it was cool and green with the sweet light of near sunrise turning part of the green gold. Dust motes floated in shafts of golden light throughout the forest. The river was half what it had been a week ago. The water was brown and unmoving in most places. In the trees all around us, birds sang and called out. Yet for 45 minutes, as we walked the trail, we barely saw any.

It was then we reached the heron rookery. The two Great Blue Heron nestling in each nest were huge now, almost as big as their parents, and they were loud. The forest echoed with their grunts or coos or whatever it was as they fussed when their parents got near. They attempted to flap their huge wings. Their large nest was certainly not big enough for the two babies and a parent.

Mario watched them for a long while. Their fussin' got on my nerves a bit. Certain noises just hurt me, especially when I haven't had much sleep. But it was perfect being out in Nature, and we didn't meet many people.

We walked over to the lake eventually, hoping to see the owl and/or the bittern. Instead the Red-winged Blackbirds serenaded us. We spotted some kind of large flycatcher. The bird ID app thought it was a Cassin's Kingbird, but I didn't hear it call out, "Come here! Come here!" which is what a Cassin's Kingbird usually says. It stayed near the top of a mesquite tree, just looking around.

We didn't see many other birds near the lake. The workers had just come in and cut the grass, so most of the birds were gone. We walked to the far end of the trail near the highway. It's darker there, and the river was running a little stronger. We almost always spot Summer Tanagers here.

It didn't take long until I saw what looked like a puffy male Summer Tanager. It seemed a little shyer than other Summer Tanagers. Later the bird identification app said it was a Hepatic Tanager. It had some of the color of that tanager, but its beak was lighter, more like a Summer Tanager.

Apparently in Central and South America, there are over 300 species of tanagers! Wow. That is hard to imagine. I wonder if they are all difficult to tell apart, like the

Summer and Hepatic Tanagers—or like the flycatchers.

I love it when birds stay still for a bit, so I can observe them and photograph them. These woods are filled with birds, yet I hardly see any. I know they are there because I hear them.

The bird ID app said it heard an Elegant Trogon. We did not hear or see it.

Vermilion Flycatcher

On the way out when we were on the unshaded dirt path, I spotted a female Blue Grosbeak in a small tree. I was thrilled. I had been waiting nearly a year to see another Blue Grosbeak. I figured there had to be a male close-by, and soon enough, he showed up. They are one of my favorite birds. I wish we had them on the Sanctuary. I am so tempted to put out a bird feeder just so I would get grosbeaks, but a bird feeder would also draw rodents and we don't need any more of them!

I had so much fun watching and taking photos of the Blue Grosbeaks. The sun was wicked hot this morning, though, almost painful, so we hurried to the car. Any day with a Blue Grosbeak is a good day.

May 31, 8:12 a.m. Pool Patio at the Sanctuary

We had planned on driving to Boyce Thompson Arboretum this morning, but I didn't sleep well, and I woke up with wicked vertigo. So I sat outside under a blue sky in a slingback chair glad to be still and not have the room spinning.

I mostly watched the Hooded Orioles that were coming and going from the palm tree. The females weave these amazing nests mostly from thread they've stripped from palm tree leaves (at least in our yard). The bird books say they make these nests in a few days. But ours have been working on their nests for a couple of years now. They built two about two years ago and never used them. In fact, we never saw a male here for those years. Now we have plenty of males, but the females still seem to be building and not laying eggs. I like the nests. They look cozy: as though you could hang there all day in the shade in sight of the blue sky. Ahhh. Like your own protected hammock.

We heard quite a few birds, but we didn't see a lot. That's OK. It was good to be outside. Hoping tomorrow the vertigo is gone.

June 1, 6:13 a.m. Boyce Thompson Arboretum, Superior, Arizona

At 4:00 a.m. we left for Boyce Thompson Arboretum. It was a nice drive, and we arrived two hours later, just as they opened. We walked their Curandero Trail first, their version of a medicinal garden. Then we headed for the tall trees—the eucalyptus and pine trees. We heard so many birds! But once again, we saw few of them, except some hummingbirds who moved so fast we could only tell they were hummingbirds.

We kept hearing Indigo Buntings. We wanted to see the IBs! They are so beautiful. We tried following their song, but we still didn't see any. It felt almost diabolical. We

Ladder-backed Woodpecker

would hear the Indigo Bunting, follow the sound, and see nothing. Then hear it again, or another one, and follow the sound: and find nothing.

We saw at least a dozen bird nests. Why do we have so few nests at the Sanctuary? Are the birds not nesting there or are we just not seeing them? The nests we saw at the arboretum were out in the open—we had no problem spotting them.

We were almost alone in the arboretum for an hour and a half: just us and the birds. But then the staff began driving very quickly down the path, raising up all kinds of dust. It was very frustrating: not seeing the birds and trying to avoid inhaling dirt and dust.

We spent some time in one of the labyrinths. We heard a Cooper's Hawk—

along with at least one Indigo Bunting and several cardinals. We actually saw the cardinals. It was lovely sitting on a bench looking out at the sun-dappled labyrinth, tall trees surrounding us. In the distance, we could see one of the rock outcroppings along with several saguaro. A perfect desert morning.

We stayed in the arboretum about three hours. We enjoyed the tall shade-giving trees. We loved the symphony provided by the birds: We only wished we had seen more.

June 2, 2023, 6:30 a.m. Patagonia, Arizona, along Sonoita Creek

Mario and I both wanted to see how the hummingbird nest was doing.

It was much colder than expected—and we loved it. To be in southern Arizona in June and need a jacket at any time of the night or day is wonderful and unexpected. Someone had cut some of the grass, so the paths were still passable. We were glad to start the Bird Hour.

Birds were everywhere. We heard more than we saw, but it was better than yesterday. We didn't find the owlets. Yet we spotted a Yellow-breasted Chat along the trail, watching us as we watched it. A couple of Abert's

Towhee dug around in the leafy path. Several Yellow Warblers flew from tree to tree, like tiny suns in the dark forest. Male Vermillion Flycatchers perched on the ends of leafless branches, so bright red I bet they could be seen from space, even as tiny as they are. Gila Woodpeckers alarmed on something—

Hooded Oriole

maybe even us. We saw and heard several fly-catchers: a Western Wood-Peewee, Cassin's Kingbird, and a Dusky-capped Flycatcher—or one like it. The bird iden-tification app said an In-digo Bunting was in the area, but we didn't see it.

As the sun rose, it burned off the chill. We stopped by the sapling with the humming-bird nest. No bird sat on the nest, so I quickly took a photo again with my phone.

Only one egg. And something else was in the nest. A baby? We couldn't tell if it was dead or alive. I texted the photo to my sister who has experience with birds and asked her if she thought the bird was dead or alive. She said the mother would have thrown it out of the nest if it was dead. So . . . here's hoping. The hummingbird came back while we were there and sat on the nest.

We continued down the trail and around the corner to the raven's nest. As soon as we neared the tree, a raven flew toward it, carrying something white in its mouth. We could hear the nestlings calling out in anticipation. We could see that they were looking more and more like real birds.

As we began walking back, I said, "How come birds and other animals know how to make babies and take care of them and people don't?" In so many ways, it seems that animals are smarter than we are. Humans have to be taught so many things.

We stopped at the Gulch at Empire Ranch on the way home. The cows have trampled the shit out of it, but it still has a certain magic.

As I was crossing the stream, I made the mistake of looking down, and I lost my balance. My right foot went into the mud and water. It felt strangely comfortable. I thought of all the times I had stepped in mud when I was a kid. Our property was along a wetland—what we called a marsh growing up—and my feet were often wet with black mud. I loved hanging out in the marsh with the Red-winged Blackbirds looking for "foolish fire" and hawks.

I kept going with my wet foot.

Normally we see several tanagers in the gulch. Not today. But we were gifted with the sight of an ever-curious Yellow-Breasted Chat. And we saw a flycatcher that the bird ID app says is a Hammond Flycatcher. I'm not sure. I couldn't see the eyes to determine

whether it had an eye-ring or not. If it is a
Hammond, it's the first one we've seen. It was
a nice short stop, and it was time for home.

June 4, 6:47 a.m.
Patagonia, Arizona,
Along Sonoita Creek

We returned to Patagonia early Sunday morning. The sun was up as we stepped onto the forest trail. Golden light streamed through the trees.

Patagonia is a tiny town that sits along the Sonoita Creek between the Santa Rita Mountains (in the north) and the Patagonia Mountains (to the south). Before white settlers came, it was a seasonal village for the Tohono O'odham. It has always felt like our kind of place. We seriously considered moving here or at least getting some land, but they are building a mine nearby that will affect the quality of living and the water.

Plans on moving here are . . . over. But we want to enjoy the wildlife here as long as we can. The trail goes along the river, and most of it is treed and shady. A huge field runs between the creek trail and then a trail where the railroad tracks used to be. It is shaded as well. When one lives in the desert, one is always looking for shade and water.

We started the Bird Hour and didn't think about anything but birds. If we started to talk about anything but birds (or things in nature we encountered on the trail), the other would say, "Bird Hour, Bird Hour," as a reminder.

We saw a tiny bird in the sky going after a Gray Hawk. The Gray Hawk is so beautiful. Of course, I was rooting for the tiny bird. In general I don't like mobbing, but sometimes a bird has got to do what a bird has got to do.

We passed by where the owlets had been: no owls.

We stopped by the hummingbird nest. Momma was gone so I quickly took a photo. A baby hummer was alive inside! Momma came back, and we watched as she fed her baby. We both wondered how she is able to feed her baby without piercing it to death. It was beautiful to watch.

Raven

Momma eventually sat on the nest again. After a few minutes, she moved from side to side and up and down—as if something underneath her was pushing her up. We guessed Jr. was telling mom it needed more food.

Soon enough, Momma flew off again. We could see the exquisitely *tiny* head of the baby hummer moving in the nest while Momma was gone. Something so beautiful about it all—and a bit horrifying: baby birds always look so icky before they get feathers, like something out of a horror movie. Tiny bodies with big weird mouths.

We felt so lucky to witness all of this.

We walked down the path to the tree with the raven nest in it. We could see two of the nestlings—maybe that's all that's there. They have feathers now and look almost grown up except for around their beaks—and for the way they fuss when their parent nears. They open their beaks wide: "Feed me! Feed me!"

Blue Grosbeak

After we left the trail, we stopped at the Paton Hummingbird Center which is just down the road. At this time of year, I want to get as many Blue Grosbeak fixes as I can. Fortunately several of them were wandering the grounds near one of the bird feeders there.

Something about any blue bird: It just feels like happiness to see them. Funny.

June 5, 6:05 a.m. Along the San Pedro River

We always love coming here. If only everyone in the world could see it, could understand what a difference it makes to life to have water, to have a river. I mean, most people know it, but do they understand it? I'm not sure I did. I used to think that Arizona was a desert and always had been without water. In fact, most of the rivers are now dry mostly because of excessive pumping: overuse by agriculture—monoculture farming and cattle—and real estate.

Here you walk along the river and everything near it is alive. Yet fifty feet away from it, it is dry and does not hold as much life—

because the River isn't what it was and the ground water is certainly not what it was.

But it was time for the Bird Hour. We watched and listened for the birds. We breathed deeply the sighs of the trees and the songs of the birds. Deer watched us and listened with huge ears, reminding me of giant jackrabbits. We heard hundreds of birds. Maybe thousands. It was difficult to see most of them. The tall trees, the branches, the leaves: all provide good cover. Still we know we are amongst the wild things.

As we approached the heronry, we spotted a Great Blue Heron flying north above the river. We assumed it was hunting for food for the children, but it kept

Curve-billed Thrasher (*Toxostoma curvirostre*): 11". Gray to light brown. Dark yellow to orange eyes. Distinctive "whit-wheet" call. They have the most beautiful songs. Some researchers believe they never repeat their songs. Tucson Audubon says 90% of their nests are in chain fruit and teddy bear cactus. Males and females incubate and feed the babies. Will reuse nests. Non-migrator.

going. At the heronry, we could see that the nestlings were almost as big as the parents. They seemed quieter than usual. Perhaps because we were a little earlier in our hike this morning.

At the lake, we looked again for the bittern. We did see three Great Blue Herons flying above, heading west. One of them appeared to be smaller than the other two. We wondered if one was a fledgling. Great Blue Herons always look so majestic and relaxed when they fly.

The bird identification app said a Great Kiskadee was in the area. This was the second time it said it heard this bird, so perhaps it was actually here. We looked for it but didn't find it. It's apparently a loud and colorful bird: black, white, yellow, and reddish. They are Texas birds, so where we were is out of their range. They are flycatchers, though, so I'm hoping they stick around (because I love flycatchers.)

No owls today. But we saw tanagers, a Western Wood-Peewee, and Yellow Warblers. I did spot Blue Grosbeaks along the river in the bushes a couple of times, but they moved so quickly that I couldn't be certain. Fortunately I got to see a few at the feeders at the San Pedro House as we left. Love these birds.

We drove to the Charleston Bridge next. We hoped to find kingfishers. We saw one here once for a blink of an eye. Now we wanted to try again. When we lived in Washington, we were lucky to see kingfishers now and again. Sighting one of them always felt mythic—as if I were a part of a long line of women connected to the wild. Or something. I would hold my breath and watch and listen as they flew past, almost always in a hurry, chattering as if irritated with our presence. Or maybe just acknowledging us. Letting us know they noticed us: We were a part of their world. I love that idea.

Now we stood in the shade on the old bridge and looked down at the River. Standing in the shallows was a Great Blue Heron. Was this the same heron we had seen flying away when we were along the river near the San Pedro House? We watched as it stayed frozen, waiting for prey. The pose felt iconic, instructive. *See, this is how you do it. Stillness. We are both two-leggeds.* Only you can fly. *Yes. But you can soar, too.* How? I feel stuck in mud. *Ahhh. See: stillness.* I can't do that. Reality crushes me. *It's all mystery.* Mysteries are meant to be solved. I can't solve the mystery of my life. *Solved? Nothing is meant to be. Except perhaps to be made sacred.*

While the heron was still, I heard a Canyon

Painted Redstart

Wren in a nearby tree chattering. Was it alarming on us? Or just communicating? With us, with another bird, with the tree? I couldn't see it, but I could imagine it twitching. I've never seen a wren still. It wasn't their way. I'm sure if I talked to one of them, they would have something to say about twitching. *Not twitching, frowning one. Dancing. Ta da!*

The heron never moved. As we left, we heard a Blue Grosbeak, but we didn't see it anywhere. That was OK. Any day with a Blue Grosbeak is a good day, whether one is still or dancing.

June 7, 7:00 a.m. South Fork Trail, Chiricahua Mountains, near Portal, Arizona

We had heard that this area is one of the premier birding spots in the world. Wow. And only three hours from our place. We had been to the Chiricahuas before but on the west side. The South Fork trail was on the east side.

We left around 3:50 a.m. and got onto I-10 which was packed with trucks. We couldn't believe it. And the road was terrible. We drive this stretch of highway every week, but now it seemed unsafe to be going this fast. We passed a rest stop that had probably 100 trucks in it. By this time, I was feeling incredibly stressed out. We finally got off the freeway and drove down a paved road for a few miles, and then it turned to a rutted dirt road. We traveled it for about 20 miles while the sun came up. We saw four black-tailed jackrabbits run across the road. The road

Sulphur-bellied Flycatcher

was so bumpy that it triggered my vertigo. I felt sick and wobbly. Was this gonna be worth it? We talked about going back, but after about an hour, the road suddenly became paved again as we neared the small town of Portal.

At this point, I said, "There must have been a better way to get here then going down that horrible road." I was quite cranky about it.

We did find South Fork Trail, at the end of a paved road through the forest. No one else was there. The trail wound up along a rocky dry riverbed. Sycamores and pine trees towered above us. In the distance, red rock cliffs rose. We started up the trail, and then I heard a strange sound. I looked down at my bird identification app. ELEGANT TRO-GON.

"Mario!"

We hurried off the trail and stood in the rocky wash and looked up. Yep. An Elegant Trogon flew into the tree next to the sycamore. It had its back to us. It flipped its tail up and pooped a couple of times. I laughed and tried to take a photo. It flew away. We heard the unmistakable call of the Elegant Trogon. We whirled around, trying to spot it. It landed in the sycamore. It didn't stay long. We only had a moment to enjoy it. And then it was off, its call echoing off the cliffs.

All right! We saw an Elegant Trogon within minutes of arriving. What else awaited us?

Mosquitoes awaited us.

We heard some birds, but they were difficult to spot in the trees. We did see some kind of grosbeak, a yellow bird, maybe a Scott's Oriole, all in an evergreen tree.

On the forest floor, a Spotted Towhee picked through the leaves. We had never seen a Spotted Towhee before, so yay!

I saw the Blue-throated Mountain-gem Hummingbird a few times, but it went by so quickly I barely knew what it was (besides a hummingbird). I thought I spotted its blue gorget, and the bird ID app said it heard it. I got no photos of it.

After a couple of hours, we left, both vaguely disappointed by the experience. I'm not sure why. It was all beautiful. We got to see the Elegant Trogon. But the drive and the dirt road had thrown me for a loop.

When we left, we decided to stop at the nearby research station, but when we drove down the road to it, we saw a sign that warned us we were on private land. I had visions of being shot for going down the wrong road or driveway by one of my fellow Americans, so we turned back.

We went home via New Mexico, on a paved road. We stopped on the west side of the mountains, but it was hot. The only birds we saw were Acorn Woodpeckers—which are cool, but I don't need to drive halfway across the world to see them. I was ready to be home.

Today, the Bird Hour didn't do much to relax me or take my mind off my anxiety. But I did get to see the Elegant Trogon. And that's what I'll hang on to. Not every adventure turns out. Well, actually, it did turn out. We didn't end up stranded on a rutted dirt road with no phone coverage. Yay us! I know what birds would have shown up then: Vultures, nature's clean up crew.

How to Help Birds

Here are some ideas from various bird and nature organizations on how to protect birds.

1. Up to a billion birds a year die from collisions with windows. Make your windows safer by putting strips on them or do something to break up the reflections. (There are many products online if you don't want to make your own.)

2. Make your yard an oasis by providing water and growing native plants that will provide shelter, seeds, and insects for the birds.

3. Cats kill over 2.4 billion birds annually in Canada and the U.S. Keep cats indoors. Be-

sides habitat loss, cats are the greatest killers of birds.

4. Researchers estimate that agricultural use of pesticides kills 67 million birds a year. Don't use pesticides, and consider buying organic food.

5. Drink shade-grown coffee. 3/4 of coffee is grown in the sun on land where forests (bird habitat) have been destroyed. Shade-grown coffee preserves the canopy and generally uses less pesticides. (You can choose many products that are better for birds.)

6. Turn out the lights. Building lights kill more than a billion birds a year (when they run into the buildings), mostly migrants. Audubon has a program called Lights Out (and you can find out more by going there). Chicago implemented the program, and they estimate they save 10,000 birds a year!

7. Don't use so much plastic, especially plastic bags. They end up in the ocean or along beaches, and birds eat them or are caught in them, and they die.

Wood Duck

Birds We Saw or Heard or Our App Reported During Our Bird Hours

Abert's Towhee

Acorn Woodpecker

American Crow

American Goldfinch

American Kestrel

American Redstart

American Robin

American Wigeon

Anna's Hummingbird

Ash-throated Flycatcher

Baltimore Oriole

Barn Owl

Bell's Vireo

Belted Kingfisher

Bewick's Wren

Black Phoebe

Black-chinned Hummingbird

Black-headed Grosbeak

Black-tailed Gnatcatcher

Black-throated Gray Warbler

Black-throated Sparrow

Blue Grosbeak

Blue-gray Gnatcatcher

Blue-throated Mountain-
  gem

Botteri's Sparrow

Bridled Titmouse

Broad-billed Humming-
  bird

Brown Creeper

Brown-backed Solitaire

Brown-crested Flycatcher

Brown-headed Cowbird

Bullock's Oriole

Bushtit

Cactus Wren

Canyon Towhee

Canyon Wren

Cassin's Finch

Cassin's Kingbird

Cassin's Vireo

Cedar Waxwing

Common Nighthawk

Common Raven

Common Yellowthroat

Cooper's Hawk

Cordilleran Flycatcher

Crissal Thrasher

Crow

Curve-billed Thrasher

Dark-eyed Junco

Downy Woodpecker

Dusky-capped Flycatcher

Elegant Trogon

Elf Owl

Eurasian Collared-dove

European Starling

Evening Grosbeak

Flammulated Owl

Gambel's Quail

Gila Woodpecker

Gilded Flicker

Golden-fronted Wood-
  pecker

Gray Catbird

Gray Hawk

Great Blue Heron
Great Horned Owl
Great Kiskadee
Great-tailed Grackle
Green-tailed Towhee
Hammond's Flycatcher
Hepatic Tanager
Hooded Oriole
House Finch
House Sparrow
House Wren
Hutton's Vireo
Inca Dove
Indigo Bunting
Ladder-backed Wood-
    pecker
Lawrence's Goldfinch
Lazuli Bunting
Least Bittern
Lesser Goldfinch
Lucy's Warbler
Mallard

Mexican Duck
Mexican Jay
Montezuma Quail
Mourning Dove
Nashville Warbler
Northern Beardless-
    Tyrannulet
Northern Cardinal
Northern Flicker
Northern Mockingbird
Orange-crowned Warbler
Osprey
Pacific Wren
Pacific-slope Flycatcher
Painted Redstart
Phainopepla
Pied-billed Grebe
Plumbeous Vireo
Purple Martin
Pyrrhuloxia
Red-breasted Nuthatch
Red-eyed Vireo

Red-faced Warbler

Red-tailed Hawk

Red-winged Blackbird

Rock Pigeon

Ruby-crowned Kinglet

Rufous-backed Robin

Scott's Oriole

Song Sparrow

Spotted Towhee

Steller's Jay

Streak-backed Oriole

Summer Tanager

Swainson's Thrush

Thick-billed Kingbird

Townsend's Warbler

Tropical Kingbird

Turkey Vulture

Vaux's Swift

Verdin

Vermillion Flycatcher

Violet-green Swallow

Virginia Rail

Warbling Vireo

Western Kingbird

Western Meadowlark

Western Tanager

Western Wood-Pewee

White-breasted Nuthatch

White-tailed Kite

White-throated Swift

White-throated Thrush

White-winged Dove

Wild Turkey

Wilson's Warbler

Yellow Warbler

Yellow-breasted Chat

Yellow-rumped Warbler

About the Author

Kim Antieau is a writer and photographer who lives in the desert Southwest of the United States with her husband, writer Mario Milosevic. Her books include *Ruby's Imagine, Church of the Old Mermaids, Jigsaw Woman,* and many others. She can sometimes be found volunteering as a birding ambassador at the Paton Center for Hummingbirds in Patagonia, Arizona. www.kimantieau.com.